Joseph R. Plazo

MAXIMUM INFLUENCE ADVANTAGE

At a Glance:

Business and Social Success
Sleight of Tongue
Life Coaching and Executive training
Influence, Persuasion Rapport Building
Leadership and Motivation

Copyright 2006

This training manual had been created for Executive Coaching purposes by Exceed Global Limited.

This system is a derivative of Neurolinguistic Programming, sales persuasion techniques, hypnotherapy and various influence methodologies.

Joseph R. Plazo

OTHER BOOKS BY THE AUTHOR

Ph.D of Persuasion (ISBN: 0-9785922-1-2)
Lethal Tongue (ISBN: 0-9785922-2-0)
Seven Gates Objection Mastery (ISBN: 0-9785922-4-7)
PS5 (ISBN: 0-9785922-3-9)

Maximum Influence Advantage

2 Day Persuasion Workshop

JOSEPH R. PLAZO, Ph.D, MBA C|EA

Joseph R. Plazo

Joseph R. Plazo

Printed in the United States of America

ISBN **1-4196-3898-X**

On the World Wide Web at

www.Amazon.com and affiliates
www.BookSurge.com
www.Xtrememind.com (PDF copies)

Joseph R. Plazo

Joseph R. Plazo

Table of Contents

Joseph R. Plazo

ACKNOWLEDGMENTS

I convey gratitude to Dr. Bandler, John Grinder, Kenrick Cleveland, Robert Dilts, Michael Hall, Bobby Boddenheimer and Tom Vizzini for the body of research which lead to Neuro-Linguistic Programming and its derivative forms of human empowerment.

I convey my recognition to other trainers and authors whose research influenced my chosen path and contributed to the building of this manual. Dr. Cialdini definitely comes to mind.

I wish to thank my business partners Dr. Joy Barredo and Master Judith Claridades for their dynamic methods of teaching and mentoring. You created a superb ambience of learning at our workshops

I thank the lively participants of the company trainings for their feedback and refinement of this training booklet.

Applause goes to my parents Rudy and Ma. Garcia Plazo as well my siblings Therese, Val and Marlon.

Kudos to friends Thom Canon, Oliver & Macy Vigilia, Ricky Laudico, Angel Pelayo, Kristine Tioseco, Patrick Sommers, Asim Roy, Graham Hadlington, Karl Welz, Andrea Rodriguez, Ruth Morales, Sheila Paycana, Tonee Edoc, Norberto Claudio and Erico Abordo.

Salutations to Ateneo University and the University of the Philippines for building my foundations.

And of course a warm hug to my special other, my better half, Runette Lamonte. She literally lights my night sky.

Joseph Plazo

Joseph R. Plazo

Before your Empowerment

This manual presupposes that the participant bears rudimentary background knowledge in NLP and business hypnotherapy. Therefore, my goal is not to create an introductory course for total newcomers to the field. Rather, I collated practical applications of the persuasive language patterns and discuss their usage in a format usable for daily human interactions.

For those without background in NLP I am confident you will find formidable ideas that can overhaul your way of dealing with people. Practiced daily, you will discover your skill developing to the point that creating rapport with anyone will be as unconscious as breathing. Of course, it will require some preliminary reading and self-study of NLP exercises to take full advantage of it.

This book does not present totally new patterns but rather, offers an overhaul of existing patterns and enhanced by my version of how these patterns can be deployed for Persuasion in social environments.

My goal is to *make life magic*. Find your personal magic within the powerful techniques you will now unleash.

Joseph R. Plazo
Jan 2006

Advanced Influence Tactics

Most Life Coaches I've talked with assert that the quickest way to enhance the quality of your dealings with people is to maximize your skills in the use of language and its myriad patterns. This is true whether you are out to sell, to persuade, to negotiate, to convince or even to make someone fall in love with you. Language conveys thoughts and your dexterity with communications determine the outcome of your interactions.

Language mastery is vital. Step back, and now realize that it does not matter what you want to accomplish; I'm confident you will always use well-crafted statements to achieve it. You see, this world operates on the economic principle of TRADE. What we want often is in the possession of someone else. To acquire it, we must offer something in return. Negotiation facilitates this trade.

The ideal exchange occurs when there is perfect understanding and compromise between parties. Through proper negotiation, we reach a win-win situation. This doesn't cover just business! Deciding of what movie to watch, what restaurant to eat in or what toy to buy will be determined by how well the parties involved negotiate.

So it's evident: whatever you seek to achieve, deploying effective and suavely delivered language patterns will help you immensely.

I cannot say it enough. Learning language patterns is key to mastering communication, because anytime you are talking -- the statements you make, and how you deliver them, make an incredible difference. You will discover that as you easily and consciously incorporate the language patterns within this book into your daily life or begin to understand them right now… as you naturally create an unstoppable, totally dynamic new YOU.

I've launched numerous corporations since 1999 and I admit that without mastery of language I could never have reached the hundreds of clients and companies I dealt with. This skill allowed me to forge mutually beneficial arrangements at every engagement… which is necessary for long term relationships. Being concerned only with what you want and not what the other person needs dooms you from the beginning.

Right now, be conscious of yourself. As you are carrying on conversations, observe the words you use. Note how you say them. Use your words to direct encounters towards an "everyone wins" situation.

Then you win.

Joseph R. Plazo

Let's Start with Rapport

Rapport is a vital ingredient to growing any relationship. We commence any encounter by becoming as much like the other person as possible to eliminate as many differences as we possibly can between us. This creates rapport.

When you use rapport in your persuasion situations, you can:

❖ Establish liking with anyone in seconds
❖ Build trust in every relationship
❖ Send hidden signs of affection and respect
❖ Achieve personal and professional flexibility
❖ Establish deep bonds of camaraderie very quickly
❖ Know when you have made your point so you can avoid "over selling"

There are four powerful ways to create rapport. This involves Pacing (imitating) a Person's Non-Verbal Behaviour. The techniques are simple.

1. Mirroring: You copy the other person's actions as if you were looking into a mirror.

2. Matching: Left and right are reversed. (This is the opposite of Mirroring.)

3. Cross-Over: Pacing with a different part of your body.
4. Mirroring or **reflecting** what the other **person says** or feels. In other words, AGREE AGREE AGREE with their points. The time for disagreement is after sufficient relationship building has occurred,

Things You Can Match When Pacing

Whole body
> Match or mirror the other person's overall position.

Partial body
> Match any consistent behaviour, gestures, head nods, and other shifts in their moods.

Half body
> Match upper or lower portions of the other person's body

Breathing
> Match depth and/or speed of the person's breathing.

Voice
> Match tonality, tempo, volume, intensity and intonation patterns. Match the mood of the person speaking. Use their favourite words (This is especially useful for pacing over the telephone.)

What's the rational behind pacing?

When we pace, we imitate. When we imitate, we create similarity. Similarity breeds attraction and comfort.

Think of your best friends. Notice what's common about them? They're mostly like you!

Understand this now:

We like people who are like themselves.

When we share the same hobbies, viewpoints and perspectives, we tend to get close. All the more so when we dress alike, talk alike and move alike.

Pacing and mirroring is a naturally effective way to create a temporary form of similarity. It conditions the mind- at a subconscious level- that there is a subtle similarity. Therefore, liking and rapport is created.

The next time you meet a total stranger, mirror his posture, his gesture and even the way he speaks. Do it subtly. Then observe how he begins to like you within minutes!

Notes:

_____

_____

_____

_____

_____

_____

_____

_____

Unleash the Power of your Voice

Tedious speakers don't only bore the audience, they embarrass the speaker. Have you ever noticed glazed looks as you present before a crowd? Fear not. Short of throwing a song and dance number, you will now learn a single powerful trick to captivate any audience.

The secret is to enliven your voice!

I've conducted hundreds of speeches in the past and discovered that the quickest and easiest way to liven up your voice is to perk up your body language.

Let's explore three easy ways to become a more energetic, powerful communicator.

POSTURE - Sit straight or stand tall. Slumping or slouching drains the life from your voice and dulls the tone of your delivery. The audience will pick up on your apathy and begin to look elsewhere. Without energy in your voice, you will quickly fail to seize attention.

GESTURE - A secret of radio DJs is that they gesture with passion and use their bodies to express themselves… even without being seen. Listen closely to your favourite station; you can feel the energy coursing through their voice as they stab at the air or sweep a fist across the control booth. Their language is alive! Try this as you speak on the phone. Pretend you are live on air. A few expressive hand gestures should spike up your conversation.

FACIAL EXPRESSION- Do people comment on how flat your voice is? Chances are you maintain a poker face. The stiffer your lips, the duller your voice. The tighter your chin, the stuffier your delivery. Remedy the poker syndrome by exploring the entire range of expressions your facial muscles will allow. Stretch those lips! Smile broadly. Widen your eyes. Pull your cheek muscles! You will naturally and instantaneously burst with new life.

Here's an enlightening exercise to try. You will need a TV and a friend.

❖ Turn on the TV news channel

❖ Watch a few news bits keeping your face relaxed and neutral.

❖ Look into a mirror. Pretend you are mute and must express the feeling of each news story to an imaginary third person. Do this with facial expression only.

❖ Repeat step three looking at your friend. Can they identify the emotion? If not, work on your expressiveness!

More Conversational Gems

❖ LISTEN TWICE AS MUCH AS YOU SPEAK. Train yourself to speak no more than three sentences in a row. Invite others for feedback.

❖ TAKE A BREATHER. After the other person stops speaking count to three before speaking. What are the benefits? First, you get to absorb what was said and it allows you to formulate an intelligent reply. Second, you show the other person consideration. Finally, you avoid interrupting the other person who may have paused only to gather his thoughts.

❖ USE CLARIFIERS. Always ask follow-up questions before responding with your perspective. Some good clarifiers include: "How so?" or "Please elaborate your story". This gives the other person the opportunity to say exactly what they mean.

❖ PARAPHRASE. When the other person has finished speaking, tell them what you think you heard. They will appreciate your empathy.

❖ DON'T JUDGE or pass unsolicited advice. Show your empathy by murmuring phrases such as: "I see", "If I were you I would feel exactly the same way."

Vocal Ju-Jitsu

Visit the locker room at an Olympic meet and you'll notice athletes psyching themselves.

"*Like a tiger*", you'll hear onc growling to himself. "*Unbeatable!*" others will mutter with ferocity. Plcase hold your laughter at the tough-guy expressions they make.

What's with the ritual? Simple. Athletes readily understand that their mental game ultimately affects performance. A stoked runner will zip faster than a comet.

Like an athlete, you must psyche yourself up before proposing something. This allows your voice to sound persuasive and in control.

The following TriStep Vocal Technique gets the electricity in your voice arcing out to your audience.

TriStep Technique

Before you begin, identify an overwhelming feeling you'd like to convey in your talk. Examples include: "seductive", "charming", "warm", "confident", "powerful", etc.

You'll discover that any such feeling convey carries a corresponding:

- ❖ Key word
- ❖ Mental image; or
- ❖ Body language

You can now use a Key Word, an Image or a Body Language posture to create the desired feelings within yourself.

So let's assume that you want to sound warm and fuzzy.

Key Word: words which help you access a warm feeling e.g. "mother", "sunshine", "smile", "dear friend", "fuzzy bear". Repeat the key word ten times to get yourself in the mood. Observe how saying the word "sunshine" lightens your spirits!

Mental Image: e.g. visualize squeezing a fuzzy happy bear, greeting a dear friend, hugging a smiling mom. Create a vivid picture and let the emotions wash over you.

Body Language: A final way to change the sound of your voice is to shift physiology. A smile on your face puts a smile in your voice. Vibrant, expressive gestures will add vitality to your speech. Exaggerate the gestures.

Now what if you wanted to sound powerful?

Key Words: "power", "commanding", "unstoppable" and similar words bring out the masterful leader in you.

Mental Image: You can see yourself as a General dressing down the troops. No among your men meets your gaze. Or picture yourself the CEO demanding the production status from your Directors. You're the man!

Body Language: Simply adopting the pose of power brings you emotional fortitude. Stand tall and proud. Maintain an unwavering gaze. Throw your chin up and your chest out. Breathe slowly and deeply. Keep your hands clasped behind your back. A rush of confidence quickly overtakes you.

Notes

_____

_____

_____

_____

_____

_____

_____

_____

_____

_____

_____

_____

_____

Power of Words

Exude authority with your statements!

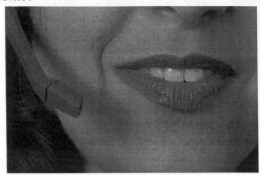

Remember the VAK- or Visual-Auditory-Kinesthetic (feelings) structure?

As we know, language patterns go beyond the auditory. Words invoke visual and kinaesthetic responses. Words create 3D movies within the minds of those who listen.

Speech connects people. Speaking allows us to share experiences that can be felt at a visceral level. These experiences can create positive effects within ourselves and others. How much more influential can you be when you share with flair?

Chomsky discussed the "deep structure of words" in his seminal work. He asserts that everything we say springs from a deep structure -- the entire gamut of feelings, emotions and experiences attached to the statements we say. Since our sentences could not possibly convey all we have in mind, it is our task to elucidate our ideas as specifically as possible to avoid misunderstanding. Ideally such SPECIFICITY, UNAMBIGUITY and CLARITY is achieved when we fully describe our experiences from a visual, auditory and feelings point of view. The next time you talk with people, do *word painting*. Speak as though you were describing a 3D entity from the palette of concrete adjectives, passionate adverbs and tangible nouns. Paint vivid pictures and your influence skyrockets.

Joseph R. Plazo

Inflection Patterns – It's How we Say it

Verbal utterances are made more effective through the use of both verbal and nonverbal conveyance. Research indicates that all communication is made up of 38% voice intonation (tone, tempo, speed, timbre) 55% physiological movements and 7% word content. Obviously, how you say things is definitely more important than what you say. People will react faster to your delivery than your content. Observe how preachers and politicians leverage this phenomenon to the hilt. Thunderous tones, melodic rhythm and emphasized promises hypnotize the audience in seconds.

The implication is clear. Mastery of language patterns requires more than perfection   of grammar and content. Statements must be spoken with the appropriate nonverbal actions and coupled with analog marking*

* refers to emphasis on some of the words in the communication. It is denoted by tonal shifts, tempo shifts, body shifts, small gestures, spatial location,

The following diagram shows the intonation patterns of interrogatives, statements, and commands.

			Word = question
Sentence	------	Last Word	/
Sentence	------	LastWord	-- Word = statement
Sentence	------	Last Word	\
			Word = command

Tag Questions

A rapid way to master the use of intonation is through the exercise of tag questions.

Tag questions are interrogatives that are employed to transform the hesitation of a question into the conviction of a statement or a command.

Tag questions are common in the English language and consist of words like *can you not?*

don't you agree? don't we? shouldn't it? wouldn't it? won't it? hasn't it? isn't that right? didn't it? can you not think that?	isn't it? hasn't it? wasn't it? aren't you? aren't they? can't you?, couldn't you doesn't it?

These words are important because we use tag questions to invite people to share our conviction by using the   intonation of a command or a statement.

Review again the yellow box above.

A **Question** has a rising intonation. The pitch of the voice climbs, marking the sentence with uncertainty. It is weak.

A **Statement** has an even intonation, making what you say appear as a declaration of fact.

A **Command** issues a falling intonation, shrouding your sentence with authority.

In order to maximize your influence and credibility, it is important to eliminate the Question Intonation from your arsenal and to utilize instead, the Statement and Command intonations.

There are two common ways you can say *"You are coming, aren't you?"*

If you raise the pitch at the end, the sentence sounds like a question begging for a decision. People can accede or disagree.

Now if you keep your pitch even , then the sentence sounds like a statement or command. You leave the person little choice other than to comply.

Try using different tonalities with questions. Observe how simply varying the pitch can transform a weak plea into a firm imperative. Begin increasing your influence and credibility by adopting the statement or command tone.

Notes

_____

_____

_____

_____

_____

_____

_____

_____

_____

_____

_____

_____

_____

EXERCISE:

Grab a personal recorder. Transform each of these sentences into
a question, a statement, and a command through the use of
intonation patterns.

Some folks like to invest in self-help classes, don't they?
- ❖ After you've listed your goals, change will easier, won't
  it?
- ❖ It's worth the effort, isn't it? You all agree, don't you?
- ❖ You have already begun to feel a shift in your confidence,
  haven't you?
- ❖ Gaining confidence is a good first step, don't you agree?
- ❖ You have learned much about yourself here, haven't you?

_____

_____

_____

Joseph R. Plazo

Joseph R. Plazo

Time Shifting
Past, Present And Future Tenses

The time distinctions of events are linguistically expressed in our language by verb tenses.

A tense denotes events as completed actions, as ongoing situations, and as something that potentially will occur. Verb tenses change our subjective experience.

Observe how your subjective experience shifts with the following verb tense changes.

1. I negotiated with him. (Past)
2. I negotiate with him. (Present)
3. I will negotiate to him. (Future)

Observe how your experience shifts with the progressive participle "negotiated,"

4. I was negotiating with him. (Past progressive)
5. I am negotiating with him. (Present progressive)
6. I will be negotiating with him. (Future progressive)

Again observe how your experiential situation shifts with the perfect verb forms of "negotiated":

7. I had negotiated with him. (Past perfect)

The past perfect tense indicates action or condition as completed at some definite past period, in relation to a past act.

8. I have negotiated with him. (Present perfect)

The present perfect tense indicates action of condition as completed or perfected in the present or having started in the past proceeding to the present.

9. I will have talked to him. (Future perfect)

The future perfect tense denotes action completed at some definite future time or taking place before some other future action. Two future events are discerned, one being further into the future than the other.

Eliminating Emotional Garbage with Tenses
Learn the secret of Life Coaches!

The previous grammar lesson provides a subtle framework that empowers you to create productive and resourceful states within people. The secret is to reorient problems and capabilities within time frames. The following illustrate.

1. A verb tense can reorient a current problem into the past by using the past tense and a tag question.

> "It had been a big problem, hasn't it?"
> "That was a bad thing you did, wasn't it?"

> *Observe how the listener suddenly loses grasp of the gravity of the problem situation... after all, the problem suddenly fades in time!*

2. A verb tense can be used for putting a present problem into the completed past by starting a sentence with the present tense and shifting to a past tense. Tag questions increase the power.

> "That is a nasty situation, wasn't it?"
> "You care to solve this dilemma, didn't you?"

3. A verb tense shifts a new and positive behavior into the future, transforms it into the present, and then looks back upon the problem behavior

"What would it be like when you have changed those bad manners now, in the future, as you look back and see what it was like to have had that situation . . . . as you consider that now?"

4. A verb tenses throws problems into the past and unleashes resources from the past, present or future.

"So, till now, you have wallowed in depression and easily, you know that you can manage it, and will do just that, if some little thing depresses you in the future, isn't that so."

EXERCISE
Write examples for the four categories of eliminating emotional garbage.

_____

_____

_____

_____

_____

_____

_____

_____

_____

_____

_____

_____

_____

EXERCISE:

1. Get a partner and use verb tenses to reorient limitations into the completed past.

> ❖ Person A states a limitation that restricts his progress.

"My friend is annoys me."
" I cannot finish this"
"I feel frustrated"

> ❖ Person B reflects the limitation in a way that states it as having long ended.

"Your friend has been annoying."
"You thought you couldn't complete it. But look, you're nearly done."
"You felt frustrated, right? But I can see you're calmer now.

What happens when problems are reframed this way? They quickly lose potency!

_____

_____

_____

_____

_____

_____

_____

_____

_____

_____

_____

_____

_____

2. List statements of limiting beliefs which presuppose a common limitation you often blame yourself for. Next to it, rewrite it in such a way that it appears as already being obsolete. BELIEVE THAT IT IS OBSOLETE.

E.g.:" I am always angry." VS "I was always angry… today I seem to be in more control"

Experience the emotional shift when a problem is reframed!

_____

_____

_____

_____

_____

_____

_____

_____

_____

_____

_____

3. Get a partner and experiment with how verb tense shifts experiences. Observe the body language and emotional change that indicate a change has taken place in the person's perceptions.

- ❖ Person A states a limiting belief and a desired solution. Person B listens and prepares to reframe what he hears.

- ❖ Person A says: "I am always procrastinating, I need motivation."

- ❖ Person B restates Person A's problems with different verb shifts, and watches for nonverbal changes in Person A. Person A offers feedback as his mind opens to new possibilities and positive outcomes

B says, "So, it **had** been a problem to get the ball rolling, is that right?"

"The way I see it, most people have found that they already had the skills necessary to motivate themselves and manage their time effectively. You simply need conscious awareness of the benefits of getting started early and finishing on time. Think about that: more free time for other things and less worries!

❖ Person A and B switch positions.

Notes:

_____

_____

_____

_____

_____

_____

_____

_____

_____

_____

Joseph R. Plazo

4. Experiment with the power of reorienting limiting beliefs into the past and moving helpful resources into the present and future.

- ❖ Person A states a limiting belief.

- ❖ "I procrastinate when the load gets heavy."

- ❖ Person B reflects the limitation by reorienting said problem into the past.

"So, you **had** been procrastinating when things look overwhelming."

- ❖ Person B then insists for a desired and positive outcome.

  - o "How **do you want** to respond to heavy loads?"

- ❖ Person A answers

  - o "Of course, to jump in with full zest!"

- ❖ Person B shifts the outcome into the present or future. He discusses possibilities!

  "So, you will feel motivated when you have that zest right now. Let me ask you... what stops you from already feeling that zest? Can you imagine how life will be whenever you blaze though heavy work and finish before the deadline? Think of all the free time you will have"

List 10 examples from this lesson.

Joseph R. Plazo

_____

_____

_____

_____

_____

_____

_____

_____

_____

_____

_____

_____

_____

_____

_____

The Power of Presuppositions

Presuppositions simply put, are assumptions.

Presuppositions are ideas taken for granted. Assumed to be true for the statement to make sense, presuppositions are rarely directly stated.

Whenever we communicate we use presuppositions that assume something is already true.

If I were to ask you: *"How much have you enjoyed reading this manual?",* you'd be hit by two presuppositions in this question. One is that you are reading this manual, and the other is that you have enjoyed it. I'm assuming both things and presupposing that both have occurred.

Here's a mortifying fact: often we do not consciously recognize what is presupposed. Our minds focus on the facts that are directly stated. Thus, the presuppositions are unconsciously and automatically accepted as being true and the listener will act as if they were true.

For instance, someone may say to you:

> "I like your work here at the company, perhaps we can get you higher responsibilities soon"

Some presuppositions include:
1) That you do good work
2) That the bosses appreciate your work
3) That others do not perform as well as you.
4) That the company rewards good work with higher responsibilities
5) That management is considering a promotion for you.

These ideas were never stated… but they are presupposed by that single statement. For this example, the presuppositions are EMPOWERING.

Now, what if the boss said, "You're an idiot and will never amount to anything."

The underlying presuppositions are grossly negative!
1) That you're stupid
2) That your work is sub-par
3) That you don't have the chance to improve
4) That promotions will never be forthcoming.
5) That you are useless.

In this case, the presuppositions disempower by creating negative, unstated assumptions of your capabilities. Watch how you presuppose things! You can quickly destroy someone's psyche with careless assumptions.

Leveraging Presuppositions for Positive Change

We habitually presuppose what we want but more often, we presuppose what we do not want. The latter can be damaging.

Here's a scheme to creating powerful change.

We can greatly increase the results we desire by **consciously presupposing what we want** and avoiding presupposing what we do not want.

A real world example for empowerment will be to presuppose that changes can be made **quickly** and **easily** or that changes will be slow and painful. Many people presuppose that change is slow and nerve-wracking. What happens??

Note how the succeeding words assume that something happens automatically or
unconsciously:

Constantly	Steadily
Automatically	Instinctively
Continuously	Involuntarily
Spontaneously	Unconsciously
Readily	Naturally, Easily

The aforementioned are presuppositions that denote the ease of doing something. They easily create a mindset leading to new possibilities.

Now sometimes, we like to presuppose that our statements are factual. We append the following presuppositions to emphasize this:

Genuine	Actual
Obviously	Actually
Authentic	Really
Self evident	Factual
Unquestionable	Absolute
Unimpeachable	True, truly
Already	Proven
Substantiated	Sure thing
Positively	Undeniably
Clearly	Irrefutable
Certainly	Definitely
Naturally	Readily

Observe how deploying such words can readily and naturally direct your mindset towards a belief of infallibility. (Note that I used presuppositions here. Did it readily get you to accept it?)

Let's take an example of sentences that use overt presuppositions.

❖ "As you sit here, learning these powerful linguistic patterns, you may **already** notice how you can **naturally** and **automatically** convince people to your ideas."

❖ "It's quite **evident** that you can certainly influence people with these **proven** techniques."

Observe how sentences sprinkled with presuppositions such as "naturally", "automatically", "proven" and " certainly" make the statement more authoritative. More convincing. The reason? Directly stated presuppositions cause the brain to jump to instant assumptions. Assumptions rarely undergo conscious scrutiny; they are accepted on the spot.

Without presuppositions, a sentence lacks compelling power. Here's a re-write without the presuppositions: *As you sit there, learning these linguistic patterns, you notice how you can convince others."*

Weak isn't it?

Bottom line: Use the presuppositive words above as often as you can to presuppose that something is EASY NATURAL or AUTOMATIC. The brain loves these words and jumps to action. Alternatively, you can also presuppose that something is FACTUAL by using words like "evidently", "obviously" and "apparently". The mind hears those words and takes the statement as gospel truth.

Remember when your doctor told you "**Evidently**, you have too much stress, as is **obvious** by your cortisol levels. I **naturally** think you must take R&R for a week, to **quickly** get you back in shape. "

His statement rings with authority as every idea is backed by powerful presuppositions. You are bound to obey.

Now had he said *"You have too much stress. I think your cortisol is too high. I recommend R&R"*

The latter statement, devoid of presuppositions, leaves questions in your mind, doesn't it? You wonder how he came to those conclusions.

Statements without overt presuppositions tend to lose its impact.

Joseph R. Plazo

EXERCISE:

(a) Write 8 sentences that presuppose something desirable in your life is happening automatically, easily, consistently…
Ex.: I automatically keep cool in times of stress

_____

_____

_____

_____

_____

_____

_____

_____

_____

_____

_____

_____

_____

(b) Write 8 sentences presupposing a desired fact. After each statement, strongly affirm these to yourself. Transform these beliefs into FACTS!

*Ex. It's evident that I have confidence around beautiful women.
I obviously learn these techniques faster than average.*

_____

_____

_____

_____

_____

_____

_____

_____

_____

_____

_____

_____

_____

We often like to suggest the perpetuity of some ideas or values.
Presuppositions of permanence come in handy for this purpose.

| lasting | unending | non-stop |
| enduring | forever | perpetual |

continuing	day after day	in perpetuity
remaining	year after year	continually
staying	everlasting	always
stable	eternal	secure
persisting	timeless	fixed
persistent	endless	indestructible
long lasting	never ending	staying power
long standing	without end	goes on and on
long term	constant	never ceases
extended	ceaseless	keeps on
stay with it		

Emphasizing corporate directives, religious values or even good behaviour can be reinforced with permanence phrases. Those who hear imperatives couched within such presuppositions find themselves compelled to perpetuate them.

Observe the following statements which make use of the language of permanence

"Now that you know you **always** had access to these capabilities, you may just begin to discover day by day all the other resources that you **already** have.

"When you stop… and realize the progress you made, you'll understand how these **lasting** changes will dramatically make your life different… and in numerous ways, far better than before."

Wasn't that empowering! Building up character is easy with presuppositions of permanence. The trick is to tell someone that they **always** had some admirable trait that everyone wishes to emulate. Even if he never had it, he will suddenly move to live up to that expectation.

Remember: expectation is a prime motivator. Think of the bandwagon effect.

Exercise:

Select 8 phrases of permanence and write down statements that you'd like to be true about yourself.
Ex. I consistently and always come on time.

_____

_____

_____

_____

_____

_____

_____

_____

_____

_____

Some things are better fleeting and temporary. Bad habits, negative attitudes and destructive behaviour are a few that we want out of our lives. We can downplay the impact of these emotional drainers by describing them with presuppositions of impermanence.

impermanence	go up in smoke	immediately
transient	melt like snow	changes
changeable	temporal	in an instant
fleeting	flitting	in no time

brief	fading	in nothing flat
no time for	here today gone	in short order
for a little while	tomorrow	like a shot
in an instant	short term	vanishes
fade away	short lived	evaporates
fade like a shadow	for a short time	replaced by
vanish like a dream	suddenly	put in place of
burst like a bubble	abruptly gone	make way for
halt	in a blink of an eye	change one's mind
stop	in two shakes	
final	momentarily	
	terminate	

Use these words to dull the impact of emotional stressors. Observe the examples that follow:

❖ "I'm sure you've already noticed how this **short-lived** problem has started to go away. It just took a bit of talking with the right people."

❖ "Mark, as you notice, this was **a momentary** setback. Now that you see things from another vantage point, the dilemma that bugged you then has now started to fade away."

❖ "Isn't it wonderful how your quarrel with Cassandra seems like an **ending nightmare** and now you're starting to talk again and finding new hope in your beautiful relationship?"

Exercise:

Select 8 of the previous words and construct statements that downplay certain black issues in your life.
Ex. I'm glad that our argument was short term and the anger vanished in a twinkling. Now we can discuss things more maturely.

_____

_____

_____

_____

_____

_____

_____

_____

_____

_____

While we have terms that presuppose something as being permanent or temporary, there are potent words that can be used to presuppose people will remember or forget something. The following chart illustrates.

REMEMBER	FORGET
lasting impression	dismiss
persist with you	think nothing of
keep in mind	lose sight of
never be forgotten	erase from memory
put in one's mind	drop from your thoughts

The usage of words of Remembrance is ideal in situations when you want to impress upon someone a value you want to be assimilated. On the other hand, you use words of Forgetting to compel a person to drop negative behaviours.

For instance:

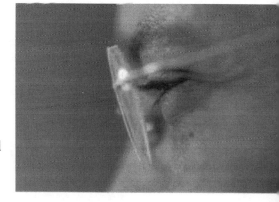

* ❖ "As you **dismiss** these thoughts clouding your head, you already begin to find new ways to tackle the problem"

* ❖ "While you **keep in mind** these good deeds, you **remember** how good it makes you feel… and how you want to keep sharing with people."

Exercise:

Select all of the aforementioned words of Remembrance and write affirmative statements that you will find useful in your area of interest.

_____

_____

_____

_____

_____

_____

_____

_____

_____

_____

_____

_____

_____

Exercise:

Select all of the aforementioned words of Forgetting and write affirmative statements that you will find useful in your area of interest.

_____

_____

Joseph R. Plazo

_____

_____

_____

_____

_____

_____

_____

_____

_____

_____

_____

_____

_____

_____

The ELEVEN Most Powerful Presuppositions in the English Language

The following structures rank among the most compelling presuppositions in the English language. While you study them, observe how they instantaneously shift mindsets and paradigms by creating assumptions that are more readily accepted. These patterns create the aura of authority by erecting pseudo-logical structures that, if not analyzed carefully, appear non-negotiable and absolute. The end result: compliance from the listener.

As you practice these patterns of authority, it will be helpful to select a specific context where you can come up with multiple phrases relevant to the situation.

I supplied sample uses of the patterns. In the following blanks, provide your own.

1. Universal Patterns
(ALL, EACH, EVERY, SOME, FEW, MANY, NONE)

> These presuppositions create massive generalizations that bypass the critical layers of our brains and ultimately leads to belief.

> ❖ "**Each** of us possesses unique skills that we can use to empower each other, don't you agree. "

❖ **"All** humans are noble." *(really? Everyone? But it's hard to disagree isn't it)*
❖ **"Everyone** deserves a second chance". *(Is that carved into stone?)*
❖ **"None** shall be left behind." *(ah... an emotional appeal)*
❖ **"Everyone** is equal."

These patterns had long been used to spout motherhood statements, political slogans, and battle cries. They inspire action because the assertion is quoted as a "universal statement" (with words like EVERYONE, ALL, NONE) Universal statements demand almost instantaneous acceptance—when someone tells you **"Everyone** deserves a just share"—you can't help but agree. Can't you?

a)

_____

_____

b)

_____

_____

c)

_____

_____

2. Temporal Pattern

(BEFORE, AFTER, DURING, AS, SINCE, PRIOR, WHILE, YET, NOW, AGAIN)

These presuppositions call upon timed-based cause and effect, thereby allowing you to create pseudo conditions that may not really exist. Used properly, these words can change people for the better.

❖ **"After** you start to use these techniques, you will realize how easy it is to influence anyone." *(really? Is there a link between realizing the ease after simply using them?)*
❖ **"Before** you master these methods, do you already notice your people skills improving?"
❖ **"During** our stay together, do you feel we can come to an arrangement?"

a)

_____

_____

b)

_____

_____

c)

_____

_____

3. Stressed Sentences

Voice stress is used on words of importance

Stressing certain words highlight the meanings behind them. Next time you issue directives, stress the important words and observe how compliance is easier to attain.

❖ "You are all ACHIEVERS who MAKE THINGS HAPPEN. Don't you AGREE with me?"

a)

_____

b)

_____

_____

c)

_____

_____

4. Ordinal Numerals

(FIRST, SECOND, THIRD, FOURTH, ANOTHER, NEXT)

Ordinal words highlight order of importance. It draws the mind to an escalation of priorities.

❖ "The **FIRST** and most important itinerary of our agenda today is to create a list of our failings"

a)

_____

_____

b)

_____

_____

c)

_____

_____

5. Adverbs and Adjective Patterns of Ease

(Easily, Naturally, Immediately, Truly, Finally, Unlimited, Already, Readily, Obviously)

> These may be the most important patterns you will ever use. When packed before the verbs or nouns they describe, these words create an irresistible attraction to the idea being discussed. Samples clarify:

❖ "Have you discovered how **easily** you can decide to work on that project right now and finish it early?" *(The assertion makes it look too easy to decide to work!)*

❖ "Have you asked yourself if the **unlimited potential** of this information is what is getting you all fired up?" *(You make the assumption that your info has unlimited potential)*

❖ "Have you **naturally** discovered how life gets better when you know how to communicate?" *(You create the assumption that its natural to discover life getting better from using those techniques)*

❖ "**Naturally,** you'll discover more reasons to proceed with this plan after you discuss with me the merits of the case." *(You imply that it's natural to discover more reasons to proceed)*

❖ "Once you begin to **easily** absorb what I'm teaching you, you'll **readily** discover how **easily** it works for you."
(You imply that it's easy to absorb the training and that it works easily)

Tip: The more of these words you pack into one sentence without sounding strange, the more magnetic your assertion will be. Ensure that the adjective or adverb is right next to the noun or adverb modified.

a)

_____

_____

b)

_____

_____

c)

_____

_____

6. Patterns of Awareness

(Aware, Realize, Experience, Feel, Perceive, Know, Understand, Conceive)

Saying any of these words makes the listener quickly start the mental process of realization that you described. These words are vital because, as with the previous pattern, everything that follows these presuppositions is assumed to be true. Most importantly, these words force the issue not whether "Will you do …", but rather, it subtly implies, "Are you aware of…."

❖ "Have you begun to **experience** the pleasure of what owning this will bring you as we discuss it?"

❖ "Do you already **realize** how reporting that to the authorities may be the right decision? " *(It is presupposed that you are aware that reporting to the authorities is the only solution. This statement is powerful because it doesn't order you to report. Rather it suggests that you know that you must report.)*

❖ **"Naturally,** as you start to **realize** the **numerous** ways we can profit from this venture, you will begin to **understand** how moving decisively right now is the only way to go."

Tip: The more of these words you pack into one sentence without sounding strange, the more magnetic your statement will be.

a)

_____

_____

b)

_____

_____

c)

_____

_____

7. Commands Pattern

(Now, Begin, Stop, Start, Continue, Proceed,)

These words compel listeners to act upon the directives couched within the statements. Obviously the best way to practice them is to begin sprinkling command patterns into your sentences as often as possible. Right NOW.

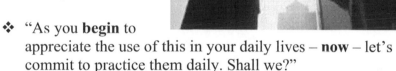

❖ "I'd like you to **stop** this waste of time and **begin** the battery of tests."

❖ "As you **begin** to appreciate the use of this in your daily lives – **now** – let's commit to practice them daily. Shall we?"

Observe how people act upon your suggestions when you BEGIN using the words "begin, start, stop, continue, proceed". Try it NOW.

a)

_____

_____

b)

_____

_____

c)

_____

8. Transformation Pattern

(CHANGE, TRANSFORM, TURN INTO, BECOME)

> Many of us like the idea of positive change. Using the Transformation Patterns, we entice the mind with tempting possibilities. This opens the listener to hearing out things that may benefit all parties.

❖ "It would be a delightful **change** if we can mobilize the team right now."

❖ "Let's **transform** this problem into an opportunity. Do you think there's a piece of gold somewhere in there?"

a)

_____

_____

b)

_____

_____

c)

_____

_____

9. Positive Adjective and Adverb Patterns

(LUCKY, FORTUNATELY, FAR OUT HAPPILY, NECESSARILY, REMARKABLE, INNOCENTLY)

> Anything that is reframed in a positive way builds up harmony. This is true whether you are talking with

others… or yourself! Harmony leads to win-win situations

* ❖ "I may be late, but **happily** she didn't notice and now I can just copy notes."
* ❖ "You are a **remarkable** person who makes me learn a lot!"
* ❖ **"Fortunately**, there's a spare even though the tire blew"

Without these positive reframes present, the sentences will weigh heavily and cause negative emotional states. Rephrase everything you state in a positive light and quickly observe how more people respond favourably. After that, try the opposite. Be negative. Then see how people run from you.

a)

_____

_____

b)

_____

_____

c)

_____

_____

10. Cause and Effect Pattern

(Causes, Because)

Here's one stealthy category!

This structure is like a virus that invades without warning; it strength draws from the fact that using Cause and Effect is a natural way that we state our beliefs. This language pattern enables you to:

❖ Use a naturally-occurring pattern to install life-changing suggestions. Covertly!
❖ Create realities of making whatever you want, cause anything else you want. This is called pseudo-logic
❖ Suggest ideas in terms of the way people form beliefs; therefore, whatever you say is more believable.

The reason this category is called Cause and Effect is that one thing can literally be said to bring about another.

As you use this technique, structure your phrase such that we have x (a pace) which happens and causes y to happen (the lead).

Use this formula to make the pattern simple:

X is a pace (something factual or directly observable)

Y is a lead (your suggestion)

Or, to simplify, ANY X can cause any Y!

Example:

❖ "Listening to me **causes** you to happily absorb what I'm saying. And, as you completely grasp it, it will **cause** you to immediately appreciate its benefits for you. " *(Do you notice a logical link between cause and effect? There is none. How does listening to me cause you to happily absorb...? Nonetheless you find yourself nodding and accepting it easily!)*

❖ "Considering your options **causes** you to agree with me

 that you need to practice this everyday. " *(This sentence tricks you into believing that merely considering your options naturally*

progresses into agreeing with me)

❖ "Simply mentioning that excuse **causes** you to accept why you already don't believe it."

How's that for under-the-radar programming! With this pattern you can get anyone to drop a bad habit. Check this out.

❖ "Smoking that cigarette the way you do **causes** you to understand how much you spend on it and how often it makes you lose breath and feel bad. Doesn't that awareness **cause** you to want to stop?"

a)

_____

_____

b)

_____

_____

c)

_____

_____

11. Implied Cause & Effect Pattern
(As...)

Another form of Cause and Effect is the "Implied Cause and Effect." It is similar in content to the previous pattern, but varies in structure. This pattern takes a milder approach.

As X (pace) happens, Y (the lead) naturally follows.

This pattern implies that two things are intrinsically linked together by some cause and effect relationship.

Examples:

- ❖ **"As** you learn this new skill and begin practicing it, you will enjoy a deep sense of satisfaction. " *(Woah! Notice how that sounded so believable. Hypnotic!)*

- ❖ **"As** you start to understand what we discussed, you will quickly think of ways how this can benefit you."

- ❖ **"As** the awareness of the advantages sink in, you'll naturally get more enthusiastic about all this."

What do you notice? Using these patterns create a compelling atmosphere of acceptance for the suggestions! The key is to link X (something already happening) with Y (something you are suggesting.) State the sentences as conversationally as you can for added impact.

Again, the formula:

As X (something that is occurring) happens, Y (your suggestion) naturally follows.

Final Example

- ❖ **"As** you smoke that cigarette, you may notice how your heart feels heavy and you just realize what a waste of time, money and effort it is."

❖ **"As** you sit there doing nothing, do you already realize how much you could be accomplishing?"

a)

_____

_____

b)

_____

_____

c)

_____

_____

Exercise

1) In pairs, experiment the use of the ELEVEN Most Powerful Phrases.

❖ Person A states a limiting belief or negative behaviour or problem
❖ Person B reframes those beliefs using the Power Phrases
❖ Both switch roles every five minutes.

2) Select important themes from one or more areas in your life and create presuppositions using any of the nine patterns that will be useful in achieving what you and others want.

_____

_____

_____

Joseph R. Plazo

_____

_____

_____

_____

_____

_____

_____

_____

_____

_____

_____

_____

_____

_____

_____

_____

_____

Joseph R. Plazo

_____

_____

_____

_____

_____

_____

_____

Why do these Presuppositions Work So Well

To convey your thoughts, you frequently speak in sentences containing a noun and a verb, hence, with each sentence you utter you actually presuppose that something exists (noun/pronoun) at some point in time. Simultaneously, you also presuppose that some action did or did not take place, is or is not taking place, or will or will not take

place.

You, as master communicators, naturally understand how to exploit this. Each time you say something, you indirectly express multiple meanings, assumptions and

overt facts. Now, you can quickly make your communication clearer and more forceful by directly stating your assumptions using the   power patterns and presuppositions. You will happily observe how authoritative your suggestions become.

Now step back and ask yourself whether you are satisfied with your current dexterity with language patterns?

No? Then the first step to proficiency is to take each language pattern and experiment with them till usage occurs at an unconscious level. The more you practice the faster you will assimilate this manner of communicating effectively. It's how I mastered the course. After you do this, you will be aware of how powerfully confident you've become.

Fortunately, learning to use these patterns is truly simple. All it takes is practice and a constant awareness of how you interact with people… whether in the bedroom or the boardroom.

Start to use these power phrases – now -- and you will find yourself inspiring, motivating, and leading people. You will mediate for them, counsel them, and enlighten them. Doesn't that excite you?

So…when could be a better time to begin extra practice than today?

> The previous paragraph had been laced with numerous power phrases. Can you spot them all?

Notes:

_____

_____

_____

_____

_____

_____

_____

_____

_____

Joseph R. Plazo

_____

_____

_____

_____

_____

_____

_____

_____

_____

Submodalities

We experience the world through our five senses known as the representation systems or modalities. The modalities include the visual, auditory (hear), kinaesthetic (feel), olfactory (smell), and gustatory (taste).

Richard Bandler, founder of NLP, asserts that the meaning of a subjective experience was directly related to submodalities. Submodalities are subsets of modalities or representation systems.

For example, in the visual modality the component elements include: whether the picture is black and white or color, how close the image is, the brightness, the location of the picture, the size, the contrast, the focus etc.

Bandler then goes on to say that as a person varies some of the submodalities, their experience will quickly change.

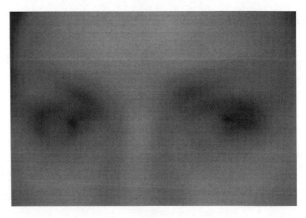

A common observation is that for most people, making a visual image of a memory closer and brighter, the intensity of the feeling attached to the imagined situation increases.

Here's the key to applying this concept. **Changing submodalities, will make major changes in experience. You can literally enhance anyone's emotions by tweaking what you say with carefully chosen words.**

The next sections of the program, provides language that may be used and "calibrated" to determine what changes are created in another's subjective experience.

The following language shifts the submodalities of space:

Submodalities of Space

Above all, that	along, with	double, up
back, to, of	between	indistinguishable
clear, of, out	condense	peak
across	amidst, among	down, to
become panoramic	beyond	inside, that, of
close down	continue forward	pick up
add more	apart, from, of	draw in
behind, all	bigger	instead of
closer	cramp	pop up
against	around	drop
below, all, that	blow over	into
come up to	disappear, from, to	putting aside
along side	ascending	duplicate
beside	bottom	keep abreast
compress	dissolve	rear
flicker, off, out	aside, from, of	dwindle
let everything drop	bring together	keep away
set at rest	distance	reduce, in size, the
from above	get clear	size
lookout over	move right ahead	expand, your
shrink it down	split	horizons keep
from behind	go back	going forward
make absent	on to	remote
shrivel it up	spread out	extend

from beneath	go behind	keep off
middle	open up	repeat, that
side by side	stop	fade away
from between	horizontal	leave it and go on
missing	overlap	replace, that
smaller	turn into	fall off
front	identical	lessen
move forward	overcome	run over
somewhere to the	immense	go by
side	overhead	opposite, to, of
halt	out of the way	stretch
outside of	terminate	go over top of
turn inside out	half, halfway	out of reach
increase	out, of, to	terminal point
past	too big	gone by
		in place of
		overlay

Examples of SubModalities of Space:

❖ "As you **observe** that, now, and **begin to rise** above all that, how manageable do you see it to be? "

❖ "As you **look** into what worried you, what new solutions **appear** to mind and give a new way of seeing it? "

❖ "You feel as if you are against the wall. What would that be like to have that **fade away**, now?"

❖ "**Amidst** all your problems are the answers you need to end them, now. "

❖ "As you **see** yourself beginning that, you may **see** your friends all around you, ready to help you, now, achieve what your goals."

Read through those statements. Feel what is said. Through the Visual Submodality, you paint emotionally touching pictures that call one to action.

Exercise:

Select a few submodalities and develop sentences that use words/presuppositions to shift submodalities of space. Use common limitations and/or responses that occur in your everyday concerns as a jump point.

❖ Person A states a limitation or a concern.

"I'd like to let you take responsibility but you are already burdened."

❖ Person B develops presuppositions that challenge the statement in a way that moves towards the desired direction.

"I'm simply requesting the opportunity to **stop** and **put aside** what we are currently doing long enough to ascertain how my taking on the added tasks can shorten the work cycle for the long term. This will **accelerate** us **beyond** our current productivity"

❖ Person A notes how this changes their experience.
❖ Person B and A switches places

Joseph R. Plazo

_____

_____

_____

_____

_____

_____

_____

_____

_____

_____

_____

_____

_____

Submodalities of Time

Words that affect submodalities of time:

abruptly	anytime now	beginning of the
from now on	in the meantime	end look
sequel	speed up	back
accelerate	as, as long as	the month that
halt	in the past	briefly
sequence	stand still	make time fly
after	as often as	the time that
here, now	instantaneously	by the time that
short term	still	mark time
ageless	as soon as	then
here today gone	keep time	carry through
tomorrow	stop	meanwhile
since	as soon as you like	thereafter
all day long	last, lately	cease
in due time	successive	moment by
soon	as surely as	moment
already	latter end	time out
in the future	suddenly	closure
span	at the same time	near future
drag on	like new	time up
over and done with	terminate	come/draw to a
during	automatically	close
pass away	live through	never
elapse	the day that	until
past	before	conclude
end	long awaited	never ending
periodic	the entire time	wait
look ahead,	beginning	consecutive
the hour that	end of the matter	newness
when, whenever	perpetually	want to
finale	endless	continuing
quickly	peter out	next time
finally	every time	for the present
reoccurrence	progressive	restart

finish	final stage	frequent
repeating	prolong	round the clock
		from day to day
		run its course

Examples

- ❖ **"Soon** enough we will prevail."
- ❖ **"After** you have taken a deep breath, you find yourself relaxed. "
- ❖ **"With** each tick of the clock, you may continue to wonderful all day long."
- ❖ "Your power grows **each day**, and your confidence becomes **endless**. "
- ❖ **"Before** you leave, you may already discover how much more delighted you are to have talked with your son… and you'd like to **continue** this again tomorrow."

Like with the previous submodality, use of this pattern excites the feelings. Teasing the emotions leads to action. Whether resultant action is positive or negative depends upon you.

Exercise:

Develop sentences using the aforementioned words to shift submodalities of time. Develop your presuppositions in response to common limitations or concerns.

- ❖ Person A states a limitation or a concern.
- ❖ Person B develops phrases that challenge the statement in a way that moves towards the desired direction.

"True, and you may also notice how **abruptly** your feeling about this transforms to something that much more pleasant because you are a naturally happy person."

❖ Person A notes how/if this changes their experience.
❖ Both Persons switch positions.

_____

_____

_____

_____

_____

_____

_____

_____

_____

_____

_____

_____

_____

_____

_____

_____

_____

_____

_____

_____

_____

_____

_____

_____

_____

_____

_____

_____

Assorted Submodalities that Tickle the emotions

act out
canceled
easy come easy go
add to the pile of
clear up
edge
at the speed of light   close
enduring
bad taste
close at hand
fade
become extinct
close down
faster
belongs to the past
concave, convex
feel yourself
blow over
crack
fine tune
boundary
crowning
flicker
make it the same
tie you in knots
close of
make no distinction
too coarse
come through
multiply
touch and go
come to nothing

break up
don't be confused
foggy
bring together
double, duplicate
for better or for worse
brink
drop
foresee
just around the corner
settled
come together
keep in mind
single
come to mind
keep in the back of your   slip away
come up against mind
slow down
standing at the edge
lapse
slower
abreast
last but one
sort out
at any rate
leave it and go on
sort what's important
at random
lies ahead

give weight to
revert to
back and forth
go by
review
back away
gradual
roll into one
black out
grinding to a halt
same for everyone
break up
hang-up
see it out
bring before
hear yourself say
see no difference
bring out
identical
see the difference
bring to mind
immense
see yourself
carry away
in the same breath
select
cast away
increase the tempo
set at rest
close in
pass by
ultimate
at a stand still
pick out
un-measurable
at the same time

never ending	from what's not	play back
turn a blind eye to	background	indistinguishable
come upon	limitless	foreground
next on the list	sounds the same	play out
turn into, turn up	turn it around	vagueness
slow down and	lingering	bit by bit
create	speed up	quicker
now or never	blow up	vanish
twinkle	look forward	breakthrough
the space	spinning	release
outlook	bring up	verge
two faced	look over, lookout	bring down
to ...	split	remain
over look	bring changes	wind-up
two-fold	lump everything	bring forward
advance	standing still	repetition
working through	bring around	without limit
come to light	together	bring to pass
return to	switch off	replay
at once	brush aside	above and beyond
come to pass	make an exception	collapse
	take a turn for the	restart
	carry out	
	make it equal	
	the last word	
	center	

These words work specifically upon the heart to break a neutral or negative frame of mind.

Examples

❖ Keep worrying about that and your world will **collapse**. Do you want that?

- ❖ Now that you know this, why don't we **speed up** your training so you can enjoy a **breakthrough** in your people skills

- ❖ Funny how memories in the past **can come forward**, and quickly change your perceptions of things today.

- ❖ As you **feel the excitement within,** you know you can hit your goals **continuously** and **without limit.** All it takes is that **endless** drive of yours.

Examples

_____

_____

_____

_____

_____

_____

_____

_____

_____

Joseph R. Plazo

_____

_____

_____

_____

_____

_____

_____

_____

_____

Criteria and How It Re-engineers Thinking

The aim of every master communicator is to target the message at the person being persuading in a way that they can't say no.

Folks like you and I have inherent "persuasion" resistance. So, your job is to present whatever you say in a way that explodes any opposition. You know you've succeeded when the person craves to hear more of your ideas and acts upon your suggestions once you pass them on.

Criteria

Another secret to influence is the use of Criteria. Without uncovering and using a person's criteria, you will fail at most communication attempts. Using this information empowers you to tailor all you say so that it has the maximal effect on that person. Instantly!

Let's see the formula.

The question to ask to elicit Criteria is:

What's important about (fill in the context) for you?

Example:

❖ *What's important about new cars to you?*

❖ *What's important about financial instruments to you?*

❖ *What's important about a piece of property to you?*

❖ *What do you look for in a guy? What traits?*

❖ *How do you shop for new appliances? What qualities are you after?*

This information is what a person uses to decide if something is good or bad. It drives a person to take action -- or to avoid it. The more closely your product or service matches the person's criteria, the more impact you'll have on this person. Always keep in mind that they're thinking:

What's in it for me?

As you promote an idea, the more you refer to their criteria and link it to your suggestion, service, or agenda, the more influence you'll have. Criteria, when properly used, can obliterate resistance.

Play it again Sam!

Once you get an answer to a criteria-mining question, remember to ask it repeatedly in different ways. Rephrase the question at least five times to obtain a "hierarchy" of criteria that you can mirror back to the listener...

and entice them with your sensitivity! People who hear you talking about their inner needs become receptive to suggestion.

Now remember this: all criteria acts to move a person towards an objective or away from a problem. This is called, for simplicity, the Towards / Away pattern. Dr. Bandler discussed that we spur a person to action by making him move toward some benefit, or avoiding some unpleasantry.

Role of Criteria

A person's personal criteria acts to move someone towards or away an idea, object or situation.

When you find that someone's criteria involves a desire to move **towards** something, you may use the following words to couch your suggestions:

get, acquire, attain, achieve, goals, include, accomplish, solutions

Now, if it's perfectly clear that he's motivated to avoid certain things, you can express your suggestions with the following words:

hide from, avoid, get away from, evade, exclude, escape, minimize.

Examples

What will having (name criteria) do for you?

Toward answers:
Q. What will having extra money do for you?
A. It will allow me more purchasing power.

Q. What will having the best quality get you?
A. I'll be proud to know I have top of the line.

Q. What will owning a Porsche do for you
A. I can confidently approach anyone.

Moving-away answers.

Q. What will having extra money do for you?
A. That I won't have to borrow from friends

Q. What will having the best do for you?
A. It's my certainty that I don't have to waste money buying again.

Q. What will having a Porsche do for you
A. Oh, it means I don't have to hide my car in a dark corner when I park.

Listen to the answer! When a person responds with Toward Answers, it is your signal to offer suggestions that imply ACHIEVING and end goal. Avoid using "moving away responses". You will alienate achievement-motivated person..

People who respond with Away-From answers are best dealt with by telling them how your suggestions make them avoid unpleasant things.

A Final Example

You: So, what are you after in brand?
Him: I like something prestigious. Armani is nice. It will get me the stares of girls

You: Okay, I'd like to recommend Armani then. Versace or Prada will be good alternatives because women are known to appreciate them.

Create your own examples. Solicit ten benefits/criteria that a friend is after. Listen carefully whether it is something they seek to gain or avoid. Craft responses that replay their criteria back.

_____

_____

_____

_____

_____

_____

_____

_____

_____

_____

_____

_____

_____

_____

_____

_____

_____

_____

_____

_____

_____

_____

_____

_____

_____

Hypnotic Language Patterns

Using Ambiguity to Empower Others

Milton Erickson was a hypnotherapist who discovered a language pattern that is artfully vague so that clients can give it meanings appropriate for any context. His pattern of conversation ultimately came to be the known as the Milton Model. It is now used in countless clinics and workshops to walk people out of destructive frames of mind and into more resourceful states. In the business world, it is a valued tool among salesmen, marketers and negotiators.

The Milton Model can be used to quickly mirror a person's reality, to distract and directionalize the conscious mind and to access the unconscious desires. From there it's a simple task of leading the person towards more productive mental conditions. It is, again, an ideal tool for Persuasion.

The following examples illustrate the Milton language patterns at play:

1. *Mind Reading*

(Statements that assert the ability to know what someone else is thinking or feeling)

❖ "I understand that you are the type who craves success. **I also know** that this training will make the sweeping changes you want to make. "

❖ "You realize that you need to improve your speaking skills. Other people felt just like you and ultimately decided to avail our services."

❖ "So many people like yourself feel that our techniques are unstoppable,"

To use this technique, you can employ the following words:

I know that you are thinking ....
You realize that ....
You understand that....
You have seen ....(visual)
You have heard that ....(auditory)
You feel that ....(kinaesthetic)

List 3 examples of mind reading statements that you can use for situations relevant to you.

_____

_____

_____

_____

_____

2. *Lost Performative*

(Statements of beliefs or standards expressed in a manner that the individual who is making the judgment or setting the standard is not identified. This way of speaking creates a pscudo-universal truth that is quite easily accepted if the listener does not actively process what is said.)

❖ **"It** will create vast and sweeping changes for you." *(What is **it**?)*
❖ **"It** has been proven that once you hire us, we can maximize your productivity and leverage your investment. "
(Who has proven it?)

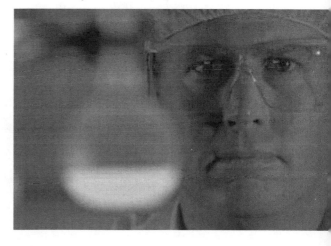

❖ **"Everyone** is quite aware that these methods of communication bring the fastest results." *(Who is **everyone**?)*

It is easy to ....
Many folks think that ....
It's been proven that ....
All the best companies ....

List 3 examples of Lost Performative statements that you can use for situations relevant to you.

_____

_____

_____

_____

_____

_____

3. Cause and Effect

(Statements that claim that there is a cause and effect relationship between one verifiable fact thing and another unverifiable fact. This structure creates a parallelism that shrouds the unverifiable fact with absolute credibility)

❖ "Taking notes in this seminar and listening to us **allows** the changes you desire in your life to happen. "

❖ "Now that are aware of your difficulty with relating, **we can begin** to help you overcome them!"

❖ "Studying this system of negotiation **quickly empowers** you to take on any challenges."

❖ "Joining us **causes** you to double your resolve."

Notice how these patterns make acceptance for your suggestions much easier. In the last example, what is the logical link between joining a group and increasing resolve? NONE! But the sentence makes it appear that joining creates an instantaneous increase in resolve. This pattern is an illustration of the power of PACING. When you pace, you state some observable fact, and link it to an unobservable suggestion. The mere link makes the suggestion look truer than it really is. Here's a good example: **"Reading these lines makes you appreciate this knowledge more and more"**. Powerful isn't it? How does reading the lines make you appreciate the knowledge? It doesn't, in reality. But I bet that you instantly appreciated those lines as your read those lines….

List 3 examples of Cause and Effect statements that you can use for situations relevant to you.

_____

_____

_____

_____

_____

_____

4. *Complex Equivalent*

(These statements imply that there is a direct connection between two totally different things. Through pseudo logic, it appears there is! Complex equivalence pertains to the equivalence we make between these two dissimilar objects)

❖ "Learning with us surely enriches your life." *(What's the connection between learning and enriching?)*
❖ "You do a great job. You must be pleased at work!" *(There may be no connection between good work and happiness at the job. But it does sound believable.)*
❖ "Your smile means you're satisfied with us."
❖ "Being in love means you'll have sex with me." *(What's the connection?? But it sure sounds believable…)*

To use this pattern, simply say "This (X) means that……."

List 3 examples of Complex statements that you can use for situations relevant to you.

_____

_____

_____

_____

_____

5. *Universal Quantifiers*

(Phrases or words that imply /state absolute conditions as being true)

❖ **"Every** person who mentored under me found an explosion of success in their life. This gives me the strength to go on serving the public."

❖ **"All** companies who have taken our services attest to our efficacy. Would you like to experience that yourself?"

❖ "Our techniques has impressed **everyone** and transformed **all** who learned. **No one** was dissatisfied"

❖ **"Everyone** can begin to feel totally relaxed, now. "

❖ **"Each time** you remember our time together, you will appreciate all I've done for you."

List 3 examples of Universal Quantifier statements that you can use for situations relevant to you.

_____

_____

_____

_____

_____

7. *Modal Operators*

(Words or phrases that signify necessity and which define the boundaries of a person's perception of reality.

You use modal operators to allow people to cross self-imposed boundaries that have long outlived any value)

Must, can, may, try, intend to, have to, should, able to, pretend to, ought to, possible to, have to, suppose to,	need to, let, allow, want to, could, permit, stop choose to, would, will, won't, decide to, wish to, got to,

Remember to match your use of modal operators with the other's personal modal operators. This creates rapport.

* "One thing is certain. To succeed at work, you **must** improve your ability to speak. We can help with that."
* "Once you **choose** to work with us, you will find yourself gaining unbelievable confidence."
* **"Do you really ought to** follow their advice? What if you don't? Make up your own mind!"
* "Why be a follower all the time? **What if you permit** yourself to speak up and take the lead?"
* **"Do** you **need** that? What **stops you from exploring** other alternatives?"

A powerful phrase that gets people thinking more positively is to ask:

"What stops you from…?"
List 3 examples of Modal Operator statements that you can use for situations relevant to you.

_____

_____

_____

_____

_____

8. Lack of Referential Index

(The use of a noun or pronoun to refer to a non specific group or category. The person doing or receiving the action is deleted. This method of patterning creates appeal to some vague authority which can, in some cases, bestow credibility)

❖ **"One** normally realizes that workshops such as this bring about empowering changes." *(Who is "one"?)*

❖ **"Everyone** agrees that mastery of negotiation is key to closing bigger deals; obviously my company is the best at providing such training." *(Who is "everyone"?)*

❖ **"It's** common knowledge that those skilled in NLP are unbeatable in the boardroom.*" (What*

exactly is common knowledge? According to whom?)
❖ **"Most** enjoy building their capacity to learn new things."

List 3 examples of referential index statements that you can use for situations relevant to you.

_____

_____

_____

_____

_____

_____

9. Comparative Deletions

(These statements do not specifically state what or how a comparison is being made. The standards by which judgments pass are vague and may allude to some authority. Marketing firms often use this technique to promote their products.)

❖ This workshop empowers you **more efficiently** than any other training offered! *(By what standards is this judgement made? The standards are deleted!)*
❖ Folks choose our services **more frequently** than the next company… and they keep coming back. *(Analyze that statement. It appears authoritative, but on a deeper level, you will wonder what exactly is meant by "more frequently". The standards are deleted)*
❖ Superb negotiators choose NLP as the bargaining tool of choice. *(Really? Who are these superb negotiators? How*

*often do they select it as the primary tool? Again, it
appears authoritative, but the criteria is deleted)*

List 3 examples of comparative deletion statements that you can
use for situations relevant to you.

_____

_____

_____

_____

_____

_____

10. Artful Pacing and Leading
(Using verbal structure to persuade)

Have you ever found yourself frustrated at convincing sceptical
clients? How would you like a magic bullet to make anything you
say sound more convincing? What about the power to enjoy
almost immediate acceptance for your proposals?

Smile. There is
away.

The secret lies
in the manner
you organize
your language -
the progression
of how you say
things and the

content that you proffer to your prospects.

The formula is easy to learn and childishly simple that it works almost all the time. With constant practice, you will find people agreeing with your every word.

A bit of history. In classical selling class, the Insurance Underwriter is taught about the 'yes set'. The theory behind the 'yes set' is that if you extract enough 'yeses' during your conversation, your prospect will automatically say 'yes' when you finally ask for the order.

Here's an illustration of the 'yes set' as taught in a fictitious insurance company.

> Underwriter: "Mr. Wakefield?"
> Prospect (Mr. Smith): "Yes. Help you?"
> Underwriter: "Mr. Richard Wakefield?"
> Prospect: "Yes."
> Underwriter: "Thank you. Mr. Wakefield, my assistant informed me that you dropped by the office last week. Is that right?"
> Prospect: "Yes."
> Underwriter: "Excellent. Can I continue?"
> Prospect: "Yes."
> Underwriter: "Sir, if I can propose to you a Pension Plan that is combination Educational Plan, Life Insurance and Accident Covered, would you like that?"

Would you feel compelled to purchase from this robotic idiot? Of course not!

But that's beside the point. What I wanted you to see was the pattern.

What did you feel as you read this little snippet? Perhaps you got annoyed at the high pressure pitch. It was too obvious! True, the salesman successfully elicited a lot of "yeses". He unfortunately did so at the cost of sounding artificial and pushy. So how can you draw out the yes-set without being this brutish? After all, you want to exude class.

The plan's simple. Unleash the power of verbal pacing and leading.

Pacing and leading creates almost hypnotic acceptance because it automatically sets up an unconscious yes-set. The technique parallels the Mirror and Match technique discussed earlier in this book.

Let's dig deeper into this method by clarifying a few terms.

The Overt Conscious:
This refers to what you are aware of in yourself and the immediate environment. It consists of the entire gamut of your thoughts, your observations, and what you see, feel and hear consist of the Conscious.

The Murky Unconscious:

This pertains to things going on all around you that you are not fully aware off. For instance, you may not be aware of your breathing. Or the beating of your heart. Or the sunlight landing on a spot behind you. Or the hotdog vendor walking along your

flank. The unconscious also refers to events that happen automatically without your cognizance. Recall the last time you played a video game and your reflexes caused you to zap almost twenty enemies simultaneously. You weren't even thinking where they are, but your fingers just seemed to 'know'!

Hence, unconscious awareness covers that which you are not aware of and that which happens automatically.

Almighty Verbal pacing and leading:

Pacing and Leading is the magical formula you're eager to learn. It's a simple yet powerful method of associating things that are true with things you'd like people to believe are true. Successfully creating this link eliminates disagreement and gets others to agree with you as a natural outcome of absorbing what you are saying.

Let's break the technique into component parts.

Pacing:

Pacing refers to discussing things that can be immediately proven to be true or things that arc commonly accepted as true.

Some examples of Pacing would be:
- ❖ The sun will rise tomorrow
- ❖ Seatbelts provide some measure of safety.
- ❖ People usually look for value of money.
- ❖ You are breathing as of this moment.
- ❖ Thoughts are possibly crossing your mind.
- ❖ You are staring at this manuscript.
- ❖ The newspaper provides news.

Now jot some of your own pacing phrases. Remember, these should be things that you have conscious awareness of and are generally seen as true.

Write 12 Pacing Examples. They should be verifiably true.

_____

_____

_____

_____

_____

_____

Leading:

Leading pertains to discussing things that you want others to accept even if they have yet to be proven or are not commonly accepted as gospel truth.

Leads are anything that you want people to believe. The following statements are considered leads:

- ❖ The best solar heater is made by ACME
- ❖ Volvo's seatbelts will save your life 100% of the time.
- ❖ Our product has best value for money
- ❖ You like to buy our product.
- ❖ Life will be better if we serve you.

What's the obvious difference between Pacing and Leading?

Pacing statements are obviously true. It's impossible to refute them as mere observation already confirms veracity. That's what makes them powerful.

Leading statements, on the other hand are not necessarily proven or may not yet be commonly recognized as true. Nonetheless, they are what you want your prospect to believe in.

So how do we bring all of this together?

Let's look at an example.

> You're looking at this paper right now, and reading these words. And as you analyze them, you already begin to

quickly understand how easy it is to convince people with this new found skill.

Whappak! Wasn't that powerful?

Let's differentiate each part:

Pace: You're looking at this paper right now *(TRUE or you won't have read it)*
Pace: and reading these words *(obviously)*
Pace: And as you analyze them *(while you read, you obviously digest the content)*
Lead: You already begin to quickly understand how easy it is to convince people with this new found skill.

Now try to use just the Lead statement alone. Delete the previous pace statements. What do you notice? The pitch takes on a hard edge; as a listener, you'll find it hard to swallow such a proposal.

Don't laugh. I'll wager you've attempted to sell with similar brutishness. Without proper prep, you jumped right towards end result you wanted-- such as, "sir, please buy this, it's a good buy". Did that work by itself? I bet it didn't.

Pacing and leading introduces a compelling difference. The previous example released three Paces before hitting the Lead statement. With each pace, the prospect's unconscious says "yes" and the beauty is that it is all so subtle that nobody thinks of it as a persuasion. Suavely, you quickly weave ambience conducive to discussion. An ambience that literally leads the other person to assent!

The Formula:

As you deploy Pacing and Leading, launch your salvo with three pacing statements followed by a lead. Please, avoid merely bouncing off a list of unrelated pacing statements. Master salesman Kenrick Cleveland suggests engaging the prospect in a dynamic conversation- make it flow nice and easy. Request for brisk responses from your prospect while selecting pacing statements that mirrors what he observes around him. You're guaranteed agreement!

> Pace Pace Pace Lead
> Pace Pace Lead Lead
> Pace Lead Lead lead
> Lead Lead Lead Lead

More examples: (Italicized sentences are the LEADS)

- You saw my ad on the papers, right? And as you checked it you found something of interest that led you to email me for more information. Now that we're talking, *you clearly look eager to join our class to improve yourself. Shall we sign you up now?*
- We've discussed how to build rapport, and also talked about the use of subtle patterns and now as you think about it, *you realize that this may be one of the most powerful human resource tools around!*
- A good diet and sensible exercise had always been suggested by doctors. Combined together, the body tends to get healthier. Since that's clear, and you're obviously after a sexy body *why don't we both enrol in the gym and switch to the South Beach diet?*
- You love comedy. I like romance. Why don't we go for both and *watch Sabrina which is a good comedy-romance.*

Create 5 paragraphs that sell an idea or product. Use at least 3 paces and 2 leads per paragraph.

_____

_____

_____

_____

_____

_____

_____

_____

_____

_____

_____

_____

_____

_____

_____

_____

_____

_____

_____

_____

_____

_____

_____

_____

_____

11. Double Binds Pattern

(Binds are statements that offer two or more choices that
are in fact the same choice)

Psychiatrists effectively
used linguistic binds for
therapeutic purposes. Its
efficacy in repressing
negative behaviour and
releasing positive
resources is well
documented.

Now, we can easily apply its use within business and social contexts to spur people into cooperative moods.

What are binds?

Binds create the illusion of choice via language that normally offers choice, where either choice you select, you still go along with what the speaker wants. Paradoxical? Not really. Later you'll soon see how often you've actually been bombarded with binds by marketers.

Binds of Comparative Alternatives

An example should quickly illuminate:

A choice is presented the prospect where "A" is choice one and "B" is choice two and "B" has the same meaning as "A " albeit worded differently.

Example

- ❖ Would you care to finalize the schedule now **or** shall we just agree when and where we'll follow this up?
- ❖ So, now that you've heard how this can benefit you, will it be MasterCard **or** Cash?
- ❖ Your children need a role model and the way I see it, you can either lead by example **or** simply walk your talk.

Let's dissect the Binds

Read the first statement and note that the first part or choice "A" is, "*finalize the schedule now*" and the second part or choice "B" is, "*agree when and where to follow this up*" Observe the difference between these two suggestions? They both mean the same thing, only worded differently. What makes the statement so powerful is the insertion of the word, "or."

Linguistically the word "or" implies the opposite. For example, if I were to write the first sentence the normal way, it might follow this theme: "*Would you like to finalize the schedule now or should we just postpone this after you think about it?*"

Now compare the original with the conventional statement. Which is more apt to achieve the goal of finalizing a meeting?

Read the two other examples, and you'll surely appreciate the use of binds for the power it will give you in contract writing, heated negotiations and even casual conversation. Your conversion rate – your success at swaying others to your viewpoint – surely jumps by leaps and bounds!

Here's the blow by blow technique.

1. First come up with a desired outcome. After that, create two different ways of saying your outcome such that either way the prospect decides, he follows your hidden agenda.

Outcome
Alternate way to say it #1
Alternate way to say it #2

Example:
#1 Would you like to attend the fancy dinner tonight
#2 Maybe we can go out later for a ritzy date?

#1 How does going through with the merger next year
#2 Lets create an alliance step by step?

2. Deliver the binds smoothly and with conviction. Link the binds with the word OR

Would you like to attend the fancy dinner tonight **or** maybe we can go out later for a ritzy date? *(Either answer, you get the date!)*

How does going through with the merger next year **or** perhaps creating this critical alliance on step by step basis sound to you?

Notice how easy it is to gain compliance to a chosen outcome! Whatever choice made, the prospect (girlfriend, client, partner), must agree with your underlying agenda.

Jot 10 examples of binding statements relevant to issues in your life!

_____

_____

_____

Joseph R. Plazo

Joseph R. Plazo

_____

_____

_____

_____

_____

_____

_____

_____

_____

_____

_____

_____

_____

_____

_____

_____

Now let's double the power of Binds.

Hidden Binds

Recall the last time someone threw a complex presentation at you, filled with jargon, disclaimers and clauses. What did you do? You demanded the bottom line just to be spared the hassle of listening anymore. It's a human response.

When a person is confused, they usually accept the first logical way out of that confusion. People are highly motivated to avoid from confusion. You can leverage this human trait.

When you use the word "or" in your binds, people trust that you will offer the opposite of the first choice. When you don't, people often go into a state of confusion

This leads to the potent hidden bind. Memorize the formula to unleash the technique:

While speaking, use a bind, but don't stop after the bind-keep talking.

Step by Step Formula

1. Identify your desired outcome.
2. Find two alternative ways of saying it.
3. Link the alternatives in a bind with "or".
2. Put it into a sentence.
3. After the bind, keep talking.
4. Use a question to "seize" a favourable response.

Examples

- ❖ I'm confident that once we end this discussion, you will either talk with your child OR spend some quality time with him. Either way, the most important thing is that you're convinced to rekindle your relationship with him. Does that feel right by you?

- ❖ That said, I don't know what you think… but whether you choose to take the trip or simply have some well deserved R&R , I feel that what's important is for you to clear your mind so you'll have enough energy for the big project next month. What do you think?

- ❖ I'm not sure whether you'll take one of our classes, or simply attend the next sampler lesson, the important thing is that you realize how communicating effectively with others will get your career flying again. Have you felt that yet?

As you link the alternatives, avoid pausing. Run through the sentences smoothly till the question. Recall what people do when they become confused? They choose the closest way out!

Hiding binds this manner creates that response. The bind vexes the mind so your prospect will accept the first logical way out.

The snappy question at the end offers an exit for the person -- by re-focusing their awareness!

Experience this for yourself. Get a friend to read the sample

sentences and pay attention to the re-focusing your experience when the question is asked at the end.

The ending question serves another purpose. It allows the bind to slip quietly into the person's unconscious as a suggestion. Your prospect need not answer the bind because its "aim" is to act as a suggestion. The whole statement loses appearance of being hard-sell!

Finally the ending question confuses the person to the point that he fails to notice that a bind was ever used. It's stealth in style!

There you have it. As you realize the power of this pattern, remember to consult your code of ethics and to manifest enough consideration on the person you employ it upon.

Now, I don't know how you plan to assimilate this into your vocal arsenal, or whether you'll enjoy practicing it in your daily conversations, what is important is that you pay attention to your expanding influence as you rise in confidence. You are having fun, aren't you?

Final Examples

❖ Would you prefer to enrol for our overview courses **or** would you like to focus on our specialized training for negotiation. Both are important aren't they?

❖ I'm confident that after our discussion you will either hire
my company or make a   decision to go ahead by
tomorrow; either way, the most important thing is that
you   become thoroughly aware of what we can do for
you. Does that sit well for you?

Give 5 examples of hidden binds drawing from contexts relevant
to you.

_____

_____

_____

_____

_____

_____

_____

_____

_____

_____

_____

_____

_____

12. *Conversational Postulate Pattern*

(This is a statement masked as a question, which when asked would require a yes or no answer. This statement is actually a stealthy command intended to incite some requested action; so whether a yes or no is given, the outcome is the same.)

- ❖ Will you pay in check **or** card to avail of our services?
- ❖ I have the papers right here; do you need a pen to sign it?
- ❖ Do you think you can understand this?
- ❖ Would it be possible for you to close that door for you?
- ❖ Can you consider taking our offer now? *(Whether you say yes or no, you ultimately accede, in principle, to taking the offer)*

Give 10 examples of questions or statements such a yes or no response leads to the very outcome you are after.

_____

_____

_____

_____

_____

_____

_____

_____

_____

_____

_____

_____

_____

_____

13. Embedded Commands Patterns

(Statements that have one or two word commands embedded within the statement itself often cause an unconscious compulsion to accede to the imperatives. Embedded commands are often stressed by use of a tonal change or a pause.)

❖ As folks like yourself, Mark, **attend our workshop** they **get excited** about how they can use the information to get ahead.

❖ When clients **hire us**, Jane, they get results and **come back** to me.

The use of embedded commands is easy. First, think of your desired outcome. Then think of phrases that elicit that outcome. Finally, insert them in a statement, and then stress those phrases as you say the statement.

Good ways to stress the command is to pause slightly before the command or to lower your accent across the phrase. The subconscious picks up on the distinction, and tends to act upon them.

Practice on your colleagues and observe how they never notice you using them!

Provide 10 sample phrases with embedded commands. Highlight the embeds.

_____

_____

_____

_____

_____

_____

_____

_____

_____

14. All Ranges of Possibilities

(Similar to Hidden Binds, This pattern announces all the options you offer to your prospect... such that all options are favourable to you. Again, consider ethics with use of this technique)

❖ When you finally decide on this Karate lesson, **I can take a check, card or cash, whatever is easy for you. I prefer cash. How would you prefer?**

❖ After you sign up for this vacation, **you can take the Shoreline Cottage, the Cliffside Manor or the Sports Accommodation. Which do you like?**

❖ It's universally accepted by our clients, our competitors and even by those who never tried our services that we are the best.

Supply ten samples of technique #14

_____

_____

_____

_____

_____

_____

_____

_____

15. Omnipotence Pattern

(These authoritative statements create the appearance that you're in full control of all possible responses to your proposals.)

The client says "How can you help us? We are unique, unlike the other guys you dealt with"

You say "Yes that is true, all firms have special needs. **And that's precisely why you should take our services because** it is our mandate to customize our packages for every company"

The client says, "I don't think this will work"
You say, "Of course not, **because I haven't told you yet what the precise benefits** are as well as the two critical factors that will have you completely convinced."

The client says, "Your manner is abrasive with the workers"
You say, "Of course **that's how I would like them to think** because I see that they need a strong leader figure. Observe how productivity has skyrocketed? No one ever comes late"

Notice that the Omnipotence pattern creates the illusion that you expected such objections and that you have well-thought contingencies for them.

Get someone to provide 6 objections. Write a response that makes it appear you expected the objection and have a ready solution.

_____

_____

_____

_____

_____

_____

_____

_____

_____

_____

_____

_____

_____

16. Grand Expectation Patterns

(Statements that create excitement and expectation are far more convincing that those that appeal to logic)

❖ When you get through this 2 minute talk, you'll see **how you can triple your revenues for just $200 by availing of our services**. Or we refund your money,

❖ How delighted **you'll be when you discover the many women you can now meet** after practicing these bite-sized methods.

❖ **In the next 30 minutes** you will unleash one of the most powerful negotiation techniques to achieve a win-win 99% of the time.

Create 12 examples of Grand Expectation Patterns relevant to your personal issues.

_____

_____

_____

_____

_____

_____

_____

_____

_____

_____

_____

_____

_____

_____

17. Open Horizons

(These statements open the mind to new possibilities while breaking down self-imposed barriers by exploring the question of What If?)

❖ "Your firm is capable of reaching the top ten company rankings in the region. **What stops you?** My consultants can guide you to that goal in less than 6 months!"

❖ "Life is constrained only by the limitations you set upon it. **What hinders you from taking the chance? What if you took the plunge?**"

We all have potentials that we are not aware of; sometimes the best way to get beyond imagined obstructions is to ask _"What stops you?"_

Solicit ten limiting beliefs from a friend and list possible eye openers to obtain a positive reframe. Say," What stops you" or "What if you could?"

_____

_____

_____

_____

18. Single Binds

(These statements link one cause to only one possible effect through pseudo logic… that nonetheless appear compelling)

More… more, more…. Less   Harder….easier,
                                    faster…slower;

- ❖ "The **more** you use what you learned in this workshop, the **greater** the change you will enjoy."
- ❖ "The **greater** your desire to meet more women, **then the less** time you should squander before you avail of my help."
- ❖ **"The more** you resist her advice, **the more** you realize how true she is, and that you're better of following her."

- ❖ **"The more** you use these patterns **the more** you'll be able to employ them at an unconscious level. And more you practice these language patterns the less hesitation you will have with women. The less you master it, the more you will fear to meet women. So… do you see what you have to do?"

Solicit ten examples using technique #18

135

_____

_____

_____

_____

_____

_____

_____

_____

19. *It's confidential but.....*

(This pattern "covertly" makes an assertion)

❖ "It's a secret, but you might want to know that this car performs better than a Toyota at 80% of the price."

❖ "I'm not going tell you that we're the best… I'd rather you find that out yourself."

❖ "I won't say that Martha is the girl for you… It's something you'll experience in due time."

When knowledge is obtained under confidence, it is valued more than widely promulgated wisdom. Leverage the power of scarcity to increase your authority.

Create 12 examples of the Confidential Patterns relevant to your
personal issues.

_____

_____

_____

_____

_____

_____

_____

_____

_____

_____

_____

_____

_____

_____

_____

_____

Advanced Hypnotic Patterns

Cartesian Logic To Challenge Objections

The following are powerful formula challenges to an objection based on weak logic.

What would happen if you did?
What would happen if you didn't?
What wouldn't happen if you did?
What wouldn't happen if you didn't?

This manner of probing forces the prospect to question his belief and discern whether the underlying logic is valid or imagined.

For instance, someone tells you
"I can't take your course; $200 is a bit high for me"

You reply
"What if you did? The most you would lose is $200… in exchange for unlimited power with people. You'd lose $200 on a single expensive date. Why not use it for a long term investment that will get you much more dates!"

Identify 12 objections you normally use to cop out on responsibilities. Write challenges to these objections using various forms of Cartesian logic. Undermine the 12 objections with extreme prejudice!

Inductive Language Patterns

(By moving the awareness from the specific to the general or from the minuscule to the all encompassing, you invite the listener to study the big picture)

- ❖ What is the overriding motivation that gets you interested in taking this course?
- ❖ It's not just about coming home late is it? *(there's something bigger)*
- ❖ It's not simply about running for office, is it? What are you really after?
- ❖ It's not only about improving your relationships, is it? *(What's the motive?)*
- ❖ When you step back and look at it, what are the big dreams behind these daily activities of yours?

Write twelve statements using inductive language patterns. The key is to invite the listener to literally step back and look at the big picture and identify underlying meta motives.

_____

_____

_____

_____

_____

_____

Emotionally Charged Words

Certain words are emotionally charged by way of association. When sprinkled in sentences, they supercharge the statement with evocative meaning that can inspire action. Observe the following words.

utterly	freedom
powerfully	totally
charged	fully
driven	completely
justice	honestly
honor	intensely
liberation	absolutely
unstoppably	intensely

The succeeding sentence glows with electricity because of charged words:

"While you fully experience that rapture of meeting new people, do you notice that sense of freedom, of liberation... that you're no longer shy... and rather.... An unstoppable powerhouse who makes things happen! "

Make it a point to talk in WORD PICTURES. Let people see, hear, feel what you're saying as they listen to you. These delightful sound bites transform you into a compelling speaker.

Exercise:
Write out 15 statements using charged words. Flip through a dictionary and hunt for more of these words.

Joseph R. Plazo

_____

_____

_____

_____

_____

_____

_____

_____

_____

_____

_____

_____

_____

_____

_____

Stop Look and Listen!

(The word "STOP" easily halts a person's internal processing and allows you to insert alternatives that can be enriching. It's the ideal tool to gain someone's attention and divert it to productive states)

Stop and get a sense of ....
Pause a moment and imagine ....
And as you **Stop** and picture ....
Stop and realize ....
Stop and observe ....
Stop and listen to ....
If you stop and think about ....
If you were to stop and say to yourself...

After you get the listener to stop, insert your suggestions. Make your assertions ENRICHING, MOTIVATIONAL and EMPOWERING.

Example:

- ❖ **Now if you were a stop**… and consider that this vacation may help you recharge.
- ❖ **Stop for a moment**…. And understand that what you're doing may not be working.

Exercise:
When someone rambles on pointlessly, tell him to STOP… and in the pregnant pause, redirect the conversation to more useful agendas.

Create 12 examples of Stop Patterns relevant to your personal issues.

_____

_____

_____

_____

_____

_____

_____

_____

_____

_____

_____

_____

_____

Swishing Towards A Goal

(Sometimes the mere arrangement of sentences spells the
difference between empowerment and disenchantment.
When you swish, you place a negative statement between
two positive ones. Recall that the mind usually
remembers beginnings and the endings.)

Observe the opposing experience created by the order of linked
statements.

"I crave it. I can't buy it. "
vs.
"I can't buy it. I crave it. "

"I would like to learn to meet more women. I can't say the right
thing though. "
vs.
"I can't say the right thing. But I would like to meet more women.
"

"I want to start a business. I have little capital."
vs.
"I have little capital... but I want to start a business."

It's quite obvious that the latter sentences ring positively and
leave the mind open to taking affirmative action. In contrast, the
former sentences apply the brakes on seeking opportunities.

Exercise:

Choose 9 problems and write 9 statements in the proper format
that inspire positive action.

Joseph R. Plazo

_____

_____

_____

_____

_____

_____

_____

_____

_____

_____

_____

_____

_____

_____

_____

_____

Conversational Gems

Conversation is an art form. Think of it like a dance of ideas or a sparring of words. Either way, conversation must always be used to enhance relationships and build long term partnerships. For this reason, I urge the reader to apply the previously discussed patterns with the goal of serving mutually beneficial interests.

The following are helpful suggestions that can naturally enrich conversations within any situation.

- ❖ Develop your fondness for listening.
- ❖ Listen non-judgementally.
- ❖ Ask follow up questions.
- ❖ Paraphrase what people tell you to demonstrate empathy.
- ❖ Always let people see how they can benefit from your proposal.
- ❖ When confronted with irritation, annoyance or anger, always defuse the situation by listening to the person vent. Validate what is said by apologies (when necessary) and offer reparation.
- ❖ Speak with a lively voice.
- ❖ Smile through the eyes.
- ❖ Gesture frequently.
- ❖ Adopt body language conducive to communication: Smile, Open your Posture, Lean Forward, Touch the other person, Maintain Eye Contact, Nod as Someone Speaks.
- ❖ Mind your manners.
- ❖ Respect personal space.

❖ Dress appropriately.

❖ Keep a positive attitude.

❖ Don't dilly dally, go straight to the point.

❖ Deliver upon your promises.

❖ Deliver solutions that exceed expectations.

❖ Develop interest in others.

❖ Demonstrate loyalty.

❖ Demonstrate honesty.

❖ Expect success and act like you're winning.

❖ Develop a "can't-wait" state of mind.

❖ Develop a "what if" outlook on opportunities.

❖ Go for Big Hairy Audacious Goals.

❖ Be the engine of your own deliverance.

❖ Free yourself from dependence upon others.

❖ Empathize.

❖ Assume that there is some nugget of good intention behind even the worst things ever said.

❖ Stand up for yourself.

❖ Stand up for a conviction.

❖ Replace aggression with charisma.

❖ Call the attention of those who trespass your rights. Point out what you find offensive.

❖ Ask open ended questions.

❖ Accept that everyone is important.

❖ Pay attention even to the weakest in the hierarchy.

❖ Use other's names in the course of conversations.

- ❖ Act natural; but tone down abrasive flaws.

- ❖ Sing in the shower: it beautifies the timbre of your voice.

- ❖ Don't glance around when someone talks to you.

- ❖ Never say "If I were you..." (it comes off as condescending)

- ❖ Avoid saying, " Just calm down..." (did it ever work??)

- ❖ Praise with sincerity.

- ❖ Learn to approach conversations from both a logical and emotional perspective.

- ❖ Sometimes, give more credit than necessary to where it's due.

- ❖ Take the lead; be proactive.....

- ❖ While simultaneously sharing power with others.

Final Assignment

That in a nutshell, is the gist of Maximum Influence Advantage workshop. You've gone through the seminar and comprehensive pattern exercises. You've no doubt read and re-read the formulas again and again. By now, you are competent enough to face countless encounters that used to stump you. Doesn't that feel empowering?

The work begins AFTER finishing this book. I'm going to ask you to fully integrate this mode of communication into your life. You can achieve this by taking two patterns a day and using them at least 15 times within 24 hours. Experiment on friends. Loved ones. Total Strangers. Talk to yourself if that helps!

Constant practice allows a natural impregnation of the principles into your mind such that you gain unconscious competence. This system of communication becomes second nature! Let this be your goal for the next two months.

Stop… and imagine the confidence. You will find yourself responding to objections and limiting beliefs with savvy. You will propose alternatives with such smoothness that you'll shock yourself! Just think: what are the grand things you can already achieve with a mere 30% of this course?

It only takes two patterns a day. And you enjoy a lifetime of fulfilling exchanges.

Now go out there and spread your light!

Bibliography

Andreas, C., Andreas, S. :   Change Your Mind and Keep the Change. Real People Press, 1987.

Andreas, C., Andreas, S. :   Heart of the Mind. Real People Press, 1990.

Bandler, R. :   Using Your Brain For a Change. Real People Press, 1985.

Bandler, R., Grinder, J. :   The Structure of Magic 1 and 2. Science and Behavior Books, 1975, 1976.

Bandler, R., Grinder, J. :   Reframing: Neuro-Linguistic Programming and the Transformation of Meaning. Real People Press, 1982.

Bandler, R., Grinder, J. :   TRANCE-formations: Neuro-Linguistic Programming and the Structure of Hypnosis.   Real People Press, 1981.

Bandler, R., Grinder, J. :   Patterns of Hypnotic Techniques of Milton H. Erickson M.D.. Volume 1.   Meta Publications, 1975.

Bandler, R., Grinder, J., DeLozier, J. :   Patterns of Hypnotic Techniques of Milton H. Erickson M.D.. Volume 2.   Meta Publications, 1977.

Cleveland, K. :   www.MaxPersuasion.com, 2001 to 2006

Dilts, R. : Applications of Neuro-Linguistic Programming. Meta Publications, 1983.

Dilts, R. : Changing Belief Systems With NLP.   Meta Publications, 1990.

Dilts, R., Hallbom, T., Smith, S. :   Beliefs: Pathways to Health and Wellbeing.
Metamorphous Press, 1990.

Moine, D., Herd, J. :   Modern Persuasion Strategies.
Prentice-Hall, 1984.

Moine, D., Lloyd, K. :   Unlimited Selling Power.   Prentice-Hall, 1990.

The Author

Joseph Riñoza Plazo is an architecture graduate with a passion for people. He accomplished his Master of Business Administration from UP in 2002 and Ph.D from BSU in 2005. He is also an EC-Council Certified E-Business Associate and a fan of languages and psychology. At the age of 22, he launched his first company, Exceed Global Ltd.

Trained in hypnotherapy, NLP, and covert sales tactics, he's often been called a rabid persuasion aficionado.

Joseph conducts training workshops for diverse organizations -- many are pro-bono. He authored six self-help books and hundreds of internet-published articles. Spare time is not down-time: Joseph reads, airsofts and dabbles in the exhilarating world of radionics.

Joseph has one goal: to touch countless souls... and *Make Life Magic*

Contact the author at joseph@xtrememind.com and joseph@powerconsultants.net

A company registered in Delaware, USA
and London, United Kingdom

Dad and the Author (right) at a wargame

Made in the USA